A Wildlife Buffet

by Libby McCord

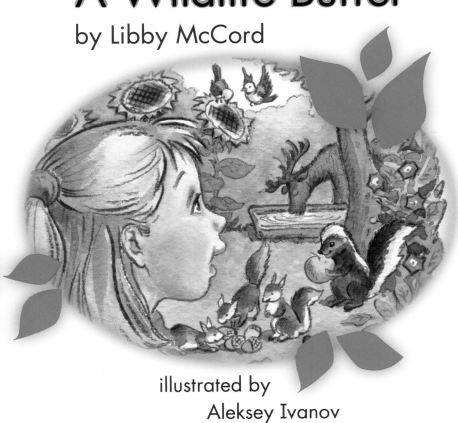

illustrated by
Aleksey Ivanov

Editorial Offices: Glenview, Illinois • Parsippany, New Jersey • New York, New York
Sales Offices: Needham, Massachusetts • Duluth, Georgia • Glenview, Illinois
Coppell, Texas • Ontario, California • Mesa, Arizona

Every effort has been made to secure permission and provide appropriate credit for photographic material. The publisher deeply regrets any omission and pledges to correct errors called to its attention in subsequent editions.

Unless otherwise acknowledged, all photographs are the property of Scott Foresman, a division of Pearson Education.

Photo locators denoted as follows: Top (T), Center (C), Bottom (B), Left (L), Right (R), Background (Bkgd)

Illustrations by Aleksey Ivanov

Photograph 12 Corbis

ISBN: 0-328-13156-3

7 8 9 10 V010 14 13 12 11 10 09 08

Cary had been waiting for Saturday, and now it was here! This was the day she and her mom would be going to the Wildlife Shelter. They were going to help with a new project.

Cary thought she would burst with excitement! She loved animals. Now she was going to do something important to help them.

Cary and her mom went inside the Wildlife Shelter. They met a man who was feeding baby birds. "How old are they?" Cary asked.

"They are one day old. We saw these birds hatch yesterday," the man said.

Cary and her mom went to join a group of volunteers.

"Welcome, everyone," said Bev. "I am Bev. I work here at the Wildlife Shelter. I am going to get you started. Let me explain what we will be doing."

"Many animals are losing their habitats. Without trees to live in or food to eat in a habitat, the animals can't survive," Bev told them. "So we are setting up a natural buffet to feed them."

"It will be like a lunchroom line!" said Cary.

"Maybe we can make strings of peanuts to feed the animals," said Cary.

"That is a good idea," said Bev. "But let me tell you about our plans." Bev brought out a large poster to show the group. "We're going to grow plants that the animals can use for food."

"We need to make sure the animals do not get used to any food they would not find in their natural habitat," explained Bev. "If they did, some birds might not fly south to find food. Some animals might not sleep in the winter. So we will only use plants that grow naturally."

Cary and the group worked hard all day. They planted many kinds of plants. When they were finished, they all felt proud of their work.

"Come see us through the summer and fall," said Bev. "Then you can see the animals eating from the buffet!"

Cary and her mom did go back.
Cary couldn't believe what she saw.
Hummingbirds drank from the morning
glories. A mouse munched berries.
Squirrels ate acorns. A deer drank
water. A skunk ate apples. Many birds
pecked at the sunflower seeds.

The buffet was a big success!

Habitats

A habitat is a place where plants and animals live. There are many different kinds of habitats. A forest is a habitat. An ocean is a habitat. A desert is a habitat. A swamp is a habitat too.

Habitats have what animals need to live. Habitats have air. Habitats have food for animals. Habitats have shelter for some animals.

This savanna is a habitat.